The Clever Tykes® Books

Change-it Cho

Illustrated by Sam Moore

For anyone who loves a challenge

Chapter 1: Slug vs Rock

"Do you really think you can beat me?" grinned Cho. She stared ahead, loosening her arms and legs. Mr Hurdle's PE lesson was ending and Cho's best friend George had dared to challenge her to another race.

"Of course I can beat you!" replied George. "You are as slow as a slug." He was already adjusting his headband and jogging on the spot. "Come on! Prepare to lose."

"Wait! I am NOT slow!" growled Cho, "and if I'm a slug, you're a..." Cho looked around for inspiration. "... a rock!" she said, spying one next to her. Cho was appalling at comebacks.

"A rock? Rocks don't move!" chuckled George.

"Exactly. You are so slow that you move as fast as a rock."

George rolled his eyes. "Are we going to race or what?"

Crouching to the floor, they both stretched out a leg behind them and looked ahead at the long, winding path to the changing rooms.

"Aha," laughed Mr Hurdle. "It looks like we have another race between George and Cho. Okay, you two. On my whistle..."

Cho glanced at George: "The slug is going to beat you, rock!"

WHEEEEEE! The whistle shrieked loudly across the school field and the two were off!

They sped past the goalposts on the field as the rest of their class cheered them on. They ran past the benches near the playground. Cho's heart was racing; she could feel energy surging through her body. She couldn't lose!

The doors to the changing rooms were in sight, but George had taken the lead.

Cho clenched her fists and ran as fast as she could. "I must win! I can't give up!" she thought as she found reserves of energy she didn't know she had.

Just then, George began to wobble and his legs jerked from side to side.

"This is my chance!" thought Cho. Her legs burned as she pushed herself harder – she was determined to overtake him.

"Woah!" George shouted. His arms spun round like a bizarre windmill.

"Argh!" cried George, tumbling along the grass.

"I – feel – dizzy!" he shouted as he rolled over and over. All Cho could do was watch him.

"Are you okay, George?" she called out, running over to check.

George was lying flat on the ground, breathing heavily but giggling.

"Wow," he panted, waving his foot in the air. "My shoelaces were undone but I'm okay though."

"Ha, I didn't expect you to be a rock AND roll," laughed Cho, feeling rather pleased with her joke.

"Yeah, yeah," said George. He brushed the grass and dirt off his shorts as Cho helped him to his feet.

"Let's go home now. School is nearly over anyway."

"I guess I win!" said Cho, who began her celebratory 'robot' dance around George.

"No way! I was in the lead!" argued George. "Gah! Not the robot again, Cho! That is too annoying."

Chapter 2: What can Cho do?

The competitive pair was still arguing about the race as they made their way home.

"We'll have to race again to decide the winner," suggested George. "I was in the lead, after all."

"Exactly, you WERE, until you started rolling around like a rock!" Cho laughed.

"I wish everyone ran as much as we did," she added, wistfully. "We could have massive races against the whole school."

"Other kids play football or computer games – everyone seems to be playing that Hunter Lion game at the moment," replied George.

Cho wanted to run for the rest of her life, even when she was an old lady. She would be the fastest old woman in the world! The villagers knew how much she liked to run and they dived out of the way when she thundered past, just so she had enough room to run on the pavement.

George chuckled and pointed across the road. "I guess those kids like eating sweets just as much as we like running!"

Cho peered over the road and saw a large group of children from school. They were all sitting on benches, munching huge bags of sweets and crisps.

"Wait a minute," said Cho in a concerned voice. "They were eating sweets yesterday, and the day before. There's something wrong about that."

*

Cho was still thinking about the sweet scoffers when she arrived home. Her dad was pretending to play guitar with a wooden spoon, while her mum swayed from side to side chopping carrots. Cho didn't mind her parents' passion for dancing as long as her friends didn't see.

"Hello, Cho!" said her mum, twirling straight into the pantry door. "Did you have a good day at school?

They were very clumsy dancers yet they always looked as if they were about to enter a dance competition. Her dad wore his best clothes every day and plucked his eyebrows weekly, while her mum's hair was always styled and she loved to wear bright jewellery. Cho, on the other hand, much preferred her running kit.

"Yeah, I had a great day at school," said Cho, staring intently at a pot of steaming broccoli.

Dad accidentally hit his knee with the wooden spoon and hopped dramatically to a stool.

"You seem quiet, Cho," he said, thoughtfully. "You're normally complaining about homework or for being told off for running in school."

"Oh yeah, sorry, Dad. I was thinking," replied Cho. "Why do you and Mum encourage me to eat fruit and vegetables?"

"Fruit and vegetables are really good for you. We want to make sure you are healthy and strong," her mum replied cheerily.

Her dad nodded in agreement. "Exactamundo! Fruit is fuel for the body. It gives you the energy and goodness you need to run quickly!"

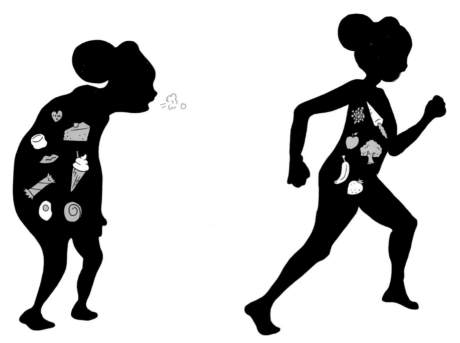

"Maybe I should tell the other kids to stop eating sweets from the shop and eat fruit instead," thought Cho aloud.

But her mum, who had been blissfully twirling around the kitchen table, suddenly came to a halt. "Oh no, dear. You can't just tell people what they can and can't do. It's okay to have treats occasionally."

"Could you imagine eating cupcakes for breakfast, lunch and dinner, every day?" added Dad. "That's a lot of sugar for your body; you could get health problems."

Cho winced at the idea "I wouldn't be able to run as fast, would I? George would beat me in races!"

Her thoughts quickly returned to the children outside the shop. They were eating sweets far too often and Cho now knew it was a growing problem.

"There must be something I can do for them," she thought.

Chapter 3: An idea is born!

"Aw, come on, let's race again. It'll take our minds off homework!" said Cho, as she and George hurried home after another day at school.

George looked hesitant. "I'm worried I'll trip over again. I think my leg needs some time to recover."

"Chicken!" teased Cho. "Your laces are tied. What are you worried about? That I'll beat you again? Are you worried that my victory dance will astound you?"

"No way! My

victory dance is way cooler!" George proceeded to jump up and down, punching the air with his fists.

Cho cringed with embarrassment: "Your dancing is just as bad as my parents'!"

Just then, they reached the shop. Cho watched in shock as she saw a girl unzip her pencil case and hide some chocolate bars inside it. A boy tucked a

bag of sweets in his socks! More were secreted between schoolbooks or even in jacket pockets.

Cho could see the children actually licking their lips as they hid more sugary snacks.

"They're sneaking sweets, George!" Cho whispered, elbowing George. "They're going to eat them in secret!"

Cho imagined the future for those children. They would become so big that they'd have to roll to the shop. There would be no more sport because

everyone would be too unhealthy to take part.

Fruit would disappear off the face of the earth and chocolate bars would become so big that they would be used to build houses instead.

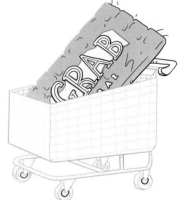

"They need to know when to stop eating chocolate, George. They need to find the balance and make sure they eat fruit, too. I have to do something," said Cho.

"Then maybe you should tell them about fruit and healthy food," suggested George.

Cho smiled and jumped onto a bench and shouted as loudly as

she could: "IT'S TIME TO SWAP THAT CHOCOLATE BAR FOR AN APPLE!"

A squirrel peered up at Cho.

"NO LONGER WILL CHILDREN EAT SWEETS EVERY SINGLE DAY!"

Her booming voice frightened a cat, which dashed into the bushes.

"I'M GOING TO CHANGE THINGS. KIDS WILL BE HEALTHY AGAIN!"

"I don't know this girl," announced George to passers-by.

He quickly pulled Cho down from the bench, eager to save his reputation. "And you think your parents are embarrassing?!"

*

At the weekend, Cho headed to the village library to learn more about healthy food. Tiptoeing across to the nutrition and food books, her trainers squeaked loudly with each step.

Miss Dorris, the librarian, tutted disapprovingly and told Cho to keep down the noise. A tall, thin woman, she wore massive glasses that made her look like a mantis. Cho was a little afraid of her fierce look.

"Sorry!" Cho whispered loudly and reluctantly took off her noisy trainers before quickly skipping to the food section of the library and hiding among the books.

Cho spent hours discovering new and exciting things about healthy and not-so-healthy food. She discovered something called a dragon fruit, and

other delicious-looking fruit that she couldn't even pronounce. They came in all colours, shapes and sizes.

"This is brilliant!" thought Cho. "I can put pictures of fruit onto leaflets and grab everyone's attention!"

She made lots of notes on her tablet computer, picking out the fun facts she thought people would like, understanding that no one would read her leaflets if they were dull and boring.

When she'd collected all the information she needed, Cho dashed past a scowling Mrs Dorris and escaped from the library, pausing only at the entrance to put her beloved trainers back on.

"Right," she said determinedly, "now let's get to work!"

Chapter 4: The shopkeeper

"Welcome home, dear!" sang her mum, who was twirling across the living-room carpet before abruptly colliding with the mantelpiece. "Oops! Did you find what you were looking for at the library?"

"Yes! I found some incredible facts about fruit. Did you know that all bananas are actually clones?" asked Cho.

"Really? Mmm, tasty!" sang her dad, who wiggled his hips into the table. "What will you do with all this new knowledge?"

"I want to change things, Dad. I really want to help my classmates to think carefully about what they eat. It's important."

"Then you should get started, Cho," said her mum. "Use what you've learned and make change happen!"

Cho ducked under her dad's flailing arms and grabbed a juicy clementine from the fruit bowl. "I'll see you at dinner!" she shouted, running up the stairs.

Cho tapped away at her laptop, designing funky leaflets that were filled with fun facts and bright, colourful pictures. She had just finished typing the last line of her leaflet when her mum called her for dinner.

After a quick victory dance, she hurried downstairs, planning how to encourage people to read her leaflet. She knew where she had to start: the very place that kids were getting their unhealthy snacks. She had to visit the shopkeeper and convince him to put her leaflets in his shop.

Later that week, Cho ventured into the village to speak to the shopkeeper. The small shop loomed before her like a great dark cave, home to the shopkeeper dragon lying in wait for its next victim.

Cho readied herself and marched into the shop, clutching a fistful of leaflets. The shopkeeper was filling his shelves with chocolate bars and sweets. He rubbed his round belly and scratched his wiry moustache, grinning wickedly.

"The children will love these new bars with popping candy AND marshmallows inside," he cackled an evil laugh and ripped open another box of chocolate bars.

"Hello, sir," said Cho, faintly.

The shopkeeper threw the empty box to the floor and spun around. His belly wobbled as he came to a complete halt. "You? I know you. You've been watching my store, haven't you? What do you want?"

Before Cho could utter a response, he snatched a leaflet from her hand. "What are these for?" His eyes darted across the words and images, his face twisted in anger.

"I want to help other children think more carefully about what they eat. Please could I put some leaflets in your shop? This is where they keep buying sweets and chocolates, after all," explained Cho.

The shopkeeper looked her in the eye, scrunched up the leaflet and threw it into the bin.

"Never!" he declared. "If you put those leaflets in my shop, you will ruin my business. Children come to buy sweets and chocolate not ridiculous fruit!"

Cho was dismayed at how mean and greedy this man was. He didn't care about children; he only cared about himself.

"You should be encouraging children to eat more healthily!" Cho went on "Why don't you have fruit in your store?"

The shopkeeper ignored Cho and pointed angrily to the doorway. "I must ask you to leave my shop. You cannot put your leaflets here, little girl."

Cho was seething.

"There has to be another way," she muttered as she stood on the pavement outside. "If I can't stop the shopkeeper from selling sweets, then I have to stop other children buying them!"

Chapter 5: Time for action!

The headteacher, Mr Holiday, was peacefully watering the petunias in his office, the sounds of ocean waves lapping at the shore playing from his computer. He was a rather timid man and this was

his moment of inner peace.

"Good morning, Mr Holiday!" came a confident voice from the door.

"Oh, my word!" jumped Mr

Holiday, spinning round and spilling water onto his desk. "Oh, it's you, Cho!"

"I would like to lead today's school assembly, please," Cho said.

"Oh, erm. This is unusual. W-what would you like to talk about?" Mr Holiday asked, quite taken aback by Cho's request.

"Healthy eating, sir!" declared Cho with a broad smile.

"Erm, well, yes, that's great, but are ... are you sure you want to do an assembly?" he asked, "You will have to talk to a lot of people."

"Absolutely, sir!" replied Cho. "I think everyone will want to listen to what I have to say about healthy food."

"Very well," agreed the headteacher. "I look forward to it, I think." As soon as Cho left, Mr Holiday returned to his plants, patting his Japanese orchid gently as if the ordeal with Cho might have worried it.

Later that morning, the school hall filled with the echoes of yawns and sighs. "Good morning!" said a jovial Mr Holiday. He was greeted with silence and blank faces.

"Well, anyway," he went on, "I would like to remind everyone that Mr Chip's Computer Club is taking place today after school – new members are always welcome!"

Some children played with their shoelaces, others tapped their fingers on their knees. Even some teachers doodled in their notebooks.

Mr Holiday cleared his throat to get their attention and told his disinterested audience: "Today, Cho will be talking to you all about something very important."

The headteacher applauded enthusiastically as Cho crept from the side of the stage. No one else clapped.

Hundreds of glum faces stared back at Cho as she peered around the hall. "I love a challenge!" she thought.

"Hey, listen up!" she shouted loudly. Everyone's head shot up as though they had just been woken by their alarm clock. A shocked teacher squeaked from the back of the hall.

Mr Holiday shuddered and wondered if he'd made the right decision in allowing Cho to take charge of his assembly.

"How many of you ate a chocolate bar or some sweets yesterday?" she asked. "I want you to be honest!"

A sleepy few raised their hands.

"Come on everyone! It's time to wake up!" said Cho confidently. Her outbursts startled Mr Holiday, and just as he approached Cho to stop her, a sea of hands rose up. Even some of the teachers had their arms raised!

The headteacher shuffled back to his chair, quietly nodding in approval. Then he, rather awkwardly, raised his hand.

Cho talked about being healthy and eating fruit. She explained why eating too much chocolate was unhealthy. People listened keenly – they all wanted to be fit and healthy.

"If you eat more fruit you will find it easier to concentrate. You will get sick less often and you'll even be able to run fast like me and my friend George! Next time you think about having a snack, make sure you *think healthy, eat healthy and be healthy*."

"Are you asking us to stop eating sweets?" shouted out one of the children in the hall. Mr Holiday was worried about this response – all he wanted was peace and calm.

Cho shook her head. "No. I am showing you what could happen if you stop eating so many sweets. It will be up to you to make the change, if you want."

All of the teachers at the sides of the hall nodded in agreement, Cho was giving the children the choice to be healthy. They weren't simply being told what to do.

"Thank you for listening, everyone. I've put some leaflets with more information by the doorway. You can even learn about strange-sounding fruit like dragon-fruit and papaya!" she said, relieved it had gone well.

Everybody in the hall clapped and cheered. George stood up in a vain attempt to start a standing ovation – Cho appreciated the effort.

"Aw, man. I want to try dragon fruit. It sounds really

cool. Do you think it means dragons are real?" asked one student leaving the hall.

"Pa-pa-pa-ya-pa-ya" uttered another. "Am I saying it right?"

Cho grinned. Were things beginning to change?

Chapter 6: The race isn't over

After a day of compliments and congratulations, Cho strolled home with George.

"You should definitely be on the TV and become a healthy eating celebrity!" George laughed.

Cho giggled, too, but as they turned the corner and spotted a group of children outside the shop again, the merriment stopped abruptly.

Cho could see something in each of their hands but it didn't have the yellow hue of a banana, nor the leaves of a pineapple. It didn't look like fruit at all.

One child reached into a bag and pulled out what looked like a lollip... Sweets! They were eating sweets!

Cho was astounded. She thought things were beginning to change. She was sure the kids at school wanted to be healthy.

Cho hurried over to them. "Hey, woah!" she cried. "Why are you eating sweets?"

"Your assembly was great," admitted one, "but you can't buy fruit in the shop or anywhere in the village – we don't have much choice!"

"Yeh, mmnom nom" chomped another boy, "we nommm ghnom mfruit hormmnom."

Cho sighed heavily and walked back to George. She knew that simply telling others to eat healthily wasn't going to be enough.

She glanced at the shop only to see the shopkeeper smirking through the dusty window. "I won't let you win," Cho scowled, staring at him.

"Come on, Cho, let's get out of here." George encouraged her away, determined to avoid any trouble with the shopkeeper.

Once they were clear of the shop, George shrugged his shoulders. "I don't know, Cho, maybe this is all too much. Maybe you should quit now."

Cho was appalled. "Quit? *Quit?* If anyone's going to quit, it's going to be ... not me! I'll have to bring fruit to the village myself!"

She began to climb a wall to begin another speech but George pulled her down.

"But Cho," interrupted George. "Won't you need permission to do that? I mean, if it was that easy to open up a stall, everyone would be selling things at the village green."

Cho decided that she needed a new plan.

Early the next day, she phoned the village hall to organise a meeting with the councillors. They would decide if Cho could make change happen!

"Oh, I'm very sorry, my dear," informed the receptionist, "the councillors don't have time to meet with children who are setting up stalls."

Cho crouched beside the phone and sank her head into her arms. It was hopeless. The children were still eating sweets and chocolate, the shopkeeper was fighting against her and there would be no meeting with the council. She couldn't to do anything without arranging that vital meeting.

Cho's dad had been doing some questionable dancing, but he stopped when he noticed his daughter looking rather gloomy.

"No luck with the council, then, sweetie? Well, you might be in luck!"

Cho frowned at him.

"I think I know someone at the council who could help," he continued. "I'll talk to him and see if we can sort that meeting for you."

Dad was on the phone for ages. The wait was exhausting but when he returned from the hallway, he looked concerned.

"I'm so sorry, Cho, but you have a lot of work to do."

Cho didn't understand. She thought he was going to arrange something.

Dad's face turned into a beaming smile: "You'll be meeting them on Friday!"

"Thank you, Dad!" She leapt into the air as her proud parents twirled beside her. He was right: she did have a lot of work to do!

Later that week, Cho started to feel nervous about the meeting. It was the same as the stomach-churning, aching feeling she got before really big races.

George saw her anxiety and grinned. "Does that mean you're going to quit?" he asked cheekily.

That comment hit a nerve and made her even more determined.

"No, I'm not going to quit, George," she smiled. "This village needs somewhere for children to buy fruit. I want to be the one to make that happen!"

Chapter 7: The make or break meeting

Late on Friday morning (after a wholesome breakfast and lots of practice, of course) Cho found herself waiting outside the council chamber.

The air was filled with the tense calm she felt at race meetings before the shot of the starting gun sounded. Eagerness surged through her body.

She imagined racing the shopkeeper, determined to beat him. She imagined him tripping over like George and rolling off the track onto his big belly. She imagined all the children at school cheering her on. She was running for them and she was going to win.

Cho took a deep breath. "All I have to do is convince the nice councillors that a fruit stall in the village is a good idea. Easy," she reassured herself. The finish line was in sight and she wasn't stopping now.

"Ah, you must be Cho. You're right on time." She was greeted by a petite receptionist who looked quite out of place in her neon orange cardigan. "The councillors are waiting for you now. Just through there."

She guided Cho to a grand old oak door. Cho took a moment to prepare. She needed to be confident and she needed to make sure this meeting was a success. This was make or break.

"Welcome to the council chamber, Cho. These are the councillors who look after the village." The receptionist introduced the councillors, one by one.

Mr Bedworth stirred from a nap when he heard his name, "Sorry, I've been travelling all night. So. Very. Tired..."

Next to him sat a middle-aged lady, Mrs Lovell, who was smiling a little too much. She squeaked with joy when the receptionist introduced her and leapt out of her chair to shake Cho's hand rapidly.

"Finally, we have Mr Hisp," continued the receptionist.

With his thin face and pouting lips, the man on the far right looked incredibly snake-like. Mr Hisp stared at his phone, failing to take notice of Cho or the others.

"I have come here today because there is something I want to change," Cho informed them. "I see students from my school eating chocolates and sweets every single day."

Mr Bedworth stretched out his arms with a wry smile on his bearded face. "Why does that concern you, young lady?"

Using the interesting facts she'd read in the library, Cho explained how important it was for children to eat healthily.

"Ah, well this may all be true, Miss Cho, but what do you intend to do about it?" asked Mrs Lovell, keenly.

"It's simple. I want to create a fruit stall to serve the children," responded Cho confidently. "Then they'll have a choice betw..."

"Pah! How ridiculous!" interrupted Mr Hisp, the first words he had spoken during the meeting. "We can't allow a mere child to run a stall in the middle of the village. Next we'll have puppies running the post

office and penguins
policing the streets.
It's preposterous!" He
hissed, glaring at Cho.

Not to be fazed, Cho
argued her case
professionally and
passionately. By the
end of the meeting, she had done all she could. The
councillors murmured amongst themselves.

"Miss Cho, could you please wait outside while we
consider your case?" Mrs Lovell showed Cho the
door and the councillors continued their discussion.

Cho sat in an old leather armchair in the waiting
room, hoping the councillors saw her as more than
just a child. She wanted to bring change to the

village – this wasn't a homework project. She wanted to make a real difference to people's lives.

Cho waited. She distracted herself by looking at all the grand paintings of former councillors adorning the walls. These were people who had all wanted to change their community. "I'll be on there one day," Cho thought.

Chapter 8: Decision time

The councillors invited Cho back into the chamber after their long hushed conversation. Mr Hisp sneered at Cho before tapping away on his phone again.

"Unfortunately, Cho, Mr Hisp is right," advised the sleepy Mr Bedworth.

Cho felt numb.

"Although you have a nice idea, you are simply too young to look after something like this. We think it would be best if you come back in a few years. When you are older we can discuss..." He went on but Cho didn't hear another word.

She was stunned. The councillors didn't care about the worries of a child and they didn't care that no one could buy fruit in the village.

Her stomach contorted. That was it – there was nothing more she could do. She imagined the shopkeeper celebrating with piles of sweets and chocolates, dishing them to out to every child.

Her hopes dashed, Cho politely thanked the councillors for their time and slowly trudged from the room.

"Sorry, my dear," whispered Mrs Lovell. Cho just nodded. She fought back tears of anger and frustration.

As soon as Cho's dad saw her shuffling down the path, he knew what had happened.

"Maybe I could take you over to George's house, he'll cheer you up. Would you like that?" asked her dad.

Cho didn't utter a word.

"I'm sorry it didn't work out, Cho. You did your best."
The two drove to George's house in a sorry silence.

*

"What?" George couldn't believe it. "They said *no?*" Cho nodded silently, staring at the ground. They were sitting on the bench in George's back garden.

"You did really well, Cho," said George, encouragingly. "I'm proud of you. Like they said, you'll just have to wait a few years and..."

"I'm not waiting" Cho murmured.

"Huh?" George frowned. "What do you mean?"

"I'm not waiting a few years, George," Cho repeated defiantly, still staring at the ground.

George's eyes widened.

"No! No, Cho, you can't!" George knew exactly what Cho was thinking.

"Yes, I can. And, yes, WE can," she said turning to look George straight in the eye. "The only way we can prove we can run a fruit stall is by doing it."

George closed his eyes in dismay. Cho's meeting with the councillors had only made her more determined. George knew she wasn't giving up just because they thought she was too young. She was going to prove

them wrong.

"I am going to set up a stall on the village green on Saturday. Are you going to be there or do I have to do this on my own?" asked Cho.

"Cho, they told you not to and we'll get into trouble!" George said as his friend continued to stare at him. "We're not doing it."

Cho held her stare.

Reluctantly, George admitted defeat.

"Argh! Okay," he agreed, finally. "I'll do it. But only for you, Cho!"

"Yes!" cheered Cho, jumping to her feet. "We've got work to do!" And with that, she marched into George's house to begin planning, leaving George sitting on the bench with his head in his hands.

Chapter 9: Change-it Cho

That Friday, Cho, her mum and dad, and George visited an orchard outside of town to collect lots of apples and pears. Despite Cho and George's frequent races and her parents' Irish dancing practice, they managed to gather all the fruit they needed for the stall. They were ready.

The next morning, when all was quiet in the village, a small secretive group shuffled down the road towards the village green.

"The coast is clear!" whispered Cho's mum, before George and Cho came speeding round the corner, carrying a kitchen table.

Dad drove down the road quietly, his car filled with the fruit.

"Operation Cho is go!" whispered Cho. "We need to be quick!"

The four of them swiftly placed all of the delicious apples and pears on display with prices. Her mum and dad were keen to share their cookery knowledge and had created some recipe guides, too!

"It needs a name!" suggested her dad, realising that 'fruit stall' wasn't catchy enough. People began to appear near the green as they started their shopping.

"No problem!" said George. He reached into his backpack and unfurled an incredible banner with the words 'Change-It Cho' emblazoned across it.

"This is your fruit stall, Cho, and I think everyone should know," he added.

"Thank you, George," said Cho. "Thanks for being here, I knew you wouldn't let me down!"

Mum handed an old megaphone to her daughter. It was getting busier as the streets filled with local villagers. "It's show time, or maybe that should be *Cho time!*"

Cho shook her head at her mum's appalling pun and took a deep breath. This was the moment she'd been anticipating for ages.

"Good morning, everyone! Welcome to the new healthy village fruit stall!" declared Cho. Her voice echoed across the village green. "Swap the sweets and make room for fruit!"

One by one, villagers wandered over to Cho's stall.

"Ooh, how very nice!" remarked a little elderly woman looking at the delicious green apples. "Can I have a bag of seven apples, please?"

"Of course!" said Cho politely, as the lady packed the apples into a bag and handed some money to George.

The two friends quickly high-fived to celebrate their first customer. As they peered around the village green, it was clear the elderly woman was going to be the first of many customers.

Teachers from school, along with members from Cho's mum and dad's dance class, approached the stall. It was going to be a brilliantly busy morning!

Mr Hurdle was quick to praise Cho's effort. "Great work, Cho! This is exactly what the village needs.

Now I can make sure the school's football team eats healthily, too!"

Mr Holiday also commended Cho. "Well, err, Cho, this is fantastic isn't it? I am very impressed with your d-d-dedication to your campaign."

Change-It Cho was inundated with praise and customers. School children appeared at the stall, excited to buy some tasty apples and pears. "Aww brill! This is going to be much tastier than another chocolate bar! Thanks, Cho!"

Out of the corner of her eye, Cho spotted the shopkeeper acting suspiciously. He held a phone to his ear and began to grin.

What was he up to?

Chapter 10: Uh-oh, Cho!

"Thank you for shopping at Change-It Cho," said George, handing a bag of pears to a young father. Cho giggled with excitement at the growing crowd. Many of them thanked her for bringing the stall to the village. Others were too busy munching on apples to say anything at all!

"There she is!" screeched a voice from across the green.

Cho looked up.

The bulbous figure of the shopkeeper stood at the far side of the grass. Cho squinted to see that he was pointing straight at her. "See? She's selling fruit! We have to stop her!"

Suddenly the serpentine Mr Hisp appeared from around the corner, and stood beside the shopkeeper. They looked furious.

"Uh-oh, Cho!" cried George. "That's a councillor, isn't it? He's coming this way! What do we do?" He began to panic.

Mr Hisp and the shopkeeper ran towards the stall, intent on stopping her, but Cho was not going to give up that easily. The race wasn't over yet!

"It's the last few minutes of sale!" she shouted into the megaphone. "Come along and grab some fruit!"

The crowd of villagers gathered tightly around the stall, with everyone clambering to buy the last bags of delicious fruit.

"Yes, get them while you can. Roll up, roll up! Apples and pears for all," shouted George.

The crowd had grown so big that the shopkeeper struggled to reach Cho. "Move out the way! I have to stop her! Stop buying her fruit!" he wheezed frantically.

Cho grinned and carried on selling fruit to the villagers. George scanned the crowd, a look of fear on his face.

"Don't look so worried, George. Look at how many people we're helping," reassured Cho.

"Well, it's just that I don't know where that councillor went."

Cho peered out across the village green. Where was Mr Hisp? Had he given up?

Suddenly a skeletal hand appeared from behind Cho and snatched the megaphone. It was Hisp! He'd slithered and slipped his way through the crowd.

The fuming councillor raised the megaphone to his mouth. Cho tried to wrestle it from him but he clutched it tightly, like a python constricting its prey.

"Attention, please," he announced in a cold authoritative voice. "Attention, PLEASE!" The crowd surrounding the stall hushed and faced Mr Hisp, who was now standing on Cho's stall. "It has come to our attention that this *girl* has started an unauthorised fruit stall in the village!"

Hisp basked in the attention. He eyed the crowd, ensuring everyone was listening.

The villagers looked up at Mr Hisp, cradling their bags that were full of Cho's fruit. Children tucked into juicy pears and licked their lips before taking a bite from an apple. Everyone was happy. This was what they wanted. They waited curiously as the councillor surveyed the scene.

The shopkeeper, on the other hand, was grinning uncontrollably, ready to claim his victory. Cho glared at Mr Hisp, her eyes filling with tears of anger. George did his best to comfort her but it was

too late. Mr Hisp and the shopkeeper were going to ruin everything.

Chapter 11 Sweet victory!

Mr Hisp gazed further into the eyes of the smiling villagers, who were grasping their fruit tightly.

He stuttered.

"Er, er... it is my duty..."

Mr Hisp was no longer his sharp, harsh self. Something was bothering him.

He paused, wiping the cold sweat from his brow. The crowd was hanging off his every word.

"Err ... It is my delight to say that the council is extremely proud to support Cho's project," he announced.

A few claps rang out from the crowd. The shopkeeper's snigger turned into a look of dismay.

Meanwhile, the councillor grew in confidence. "Yes, yes, as soon as Miss Cho brought this magnificent idea to us, we backed her all the way!" The applause grew louder and Mr Hisp broke into a smile holding a hand aloft.

Cho couldn't believe what she was hearing. She was furious that people were applauding him. How could he lie to them? How could he take the credit for this?

But slowly, Cho realised what this change of heart meant: Mr Hisp was finally allowing her to keep her stall. She'd done it!

The crowd cheered and celebrated, as Mr Hisp stepped down from his podium. He beckoned Cho over to a quieter place away from the stall.

"I'm sorry to have put you through that, Cho. Surely, you must understand that it is not easy for us adults to let children do whatever they want."

Cho nodded, still full of mixed emotions.

"Today, however, you proved that you are different. I am sorry I doubted you. You've changed this village for the better."

He handed the speakerphone back to Cho and congratulated her, before she hurried back to the stall to help George.

* * * * *

Word soon spread throughout the village that Cho would sell fruit every weekend at the village green. More customers flocked to the stall each week to buy apples and pears.

As she became more successful, Cho began to sell a variety of fruits, including strawberries, bananas and oranges. Eventually, she opened some more stalls in nearby villages and started advertising in the local newspaper and on the internet!

One morning, a cheery Mr Holiday greeted Cho with good news.

"Y-you have been invited to visit other schools! They want you to talk to the children about healthy eating."

Cho was speechless. This was even better than winning the Olympics – her healthy eating campaign was being recognised by more people!

Just as she had done at her own school, Cho stood in front of a hall filled with students at a different school.

"Hello. My name is Cho and I'm here to make a change."

THE END

Change-it Cho is the third in the series of the Clever Tykes books. We really hoped you enjoyed reading it and be sure to check out the other titles in the series.

If you'd like to learn more about the Clever Tykes books visit www.CleverTykes.com. We'd love to hear from you!

You can even send an email to Cho and tell her what you think of her story: cho@clevertykes.com

You'll find us on Facebook (/CleverTykes) and follow Clever Tykes on Twitter @CleverTykes

Written by Ben, Jodie and Jason.